To _____

From _____

Prayers for a Woman of Worth

Previously published under the title
Becoming a Woman of Worth Prayer Book

Copyright © 2015 by Christian Art Publishers
PO Box 1599, Vereeniging, 1930, RSA

Designed by Christian Art Publishers

Images used under license by Shutterstock.com

Christian Art Publishers has made every effort to trace the ownership of all
quotes and poems in this book. In the event of any question that may arise from
the use of any quote or poem, we regret any error made and will be pleased to
make the necessary correction in future editions of this book.

Printed in China

ISBN 978-1-4321-1124-3

15 16 17 18 19 20 21 22 23 24 – 12 11 10 9 8 7 6 5 4 3

PRAYERS
FOR A
Woman
OF WORTH

KAREN MOORE

CHRISTIAN ART PUBLISHERS

CONTENTS

Walking in Prayer

If we live in the Spirit,
let us also walk in the Spirit.

GALATIANS 5:25 NKJV

Heavenly Father,
When we were young, You helped us learn to walk.
You protected our steps and applauded our efforts
to grow so that we could not only walk, but run
and leap as well.

As we've learned to walk closer to You, Lord,
we've grown to trust that You are always beside us,
always near to guide and support us on the way.

You are indeed a loving friend and our
relationship with You can be as intimate and as real
as we choose it to be.

Lord, help us to choose to walk with You in all
that we do. Help us to seek Your advice and Your
wisdom for our lives. Help us to admit when we've

fallen down and need You to pick us up again.
Help us keep steadily on the path, moving always
in the direction You would have us go.

We're not as young now, Lord, but we still
come to You in childlike faith, holding out our
arms for Your kindness and Your embrace. Help
us stay close to You always, learning to trust and
obey with every step we take.

Let us walk the walk with You every moment
we live. In Your Spirit, we pray.

Amen.

Take God for your spouse and friend and
walk with Him continually, and you will not
sin and will learn to love, and the things
you must do will work out prosperously for you.

JOHN OF THE CROSS

Waiting for Him

*I wait for the L*ORD*, my soul waits,*
and in His word I do hope. My soul waits
for the Lord, more than those who watch
for the morning – yes, more than those
who watch for the morning.

PSALM 130:5-6 NKJV

Heavenly Father,

So many times we bring our requests before You, hoping for instant answers and easy direction. Sometimes You meet our needs generously and quickly and spoil us with Your great love and kindness.

Help us to understand that when we have to wait longer, when we must be patient before the answer comes, that it is not that You have withdrawn Your favor or that You delay the answer out of some desire to simply make us wait, but that You are working all things together for our good and that the process itself takes time.

Help us to always speak our hearts and minds to You with a genuine faith, believing that You want the best for us at all times. Grant that we might rest in Your Hand until the measure of our faith and the grace of Your will for us brings the blessing we hope to receive.

In all things, Lord, keep us ever mindful that You hear us and are already moving before us to answer.

Praise You, O Lord!

Amen.

We must wait for God, long, meekly,
in the wind and wet, in the thunder
and lightning, in the cold and the dark.
Wait, and He will come. He never
comes to those who do not wait.

F. W. FABER

A Woman of Wisdom

The wisdom of this world is foolishness with God. For it is written, "He catches the wise in their own craftiness"; and again, "The Lord knows the thoughts of the wise, that they are futile."

1 CORINTHIANS 3:19-20 NKJV

Heavenly Father,
Sometimes we think wisdom has something to do with being smart. We think knowledge is wisdom. We think life experience is wisdom. We think getting older is wisdom. Yet, Lord, we are not consistent in our own wisdom, our own life experience or our limited knowledge. We are wise in some things and foolish in others.

Help us to desire more fully to understand Your definition of what it means to be wise. Help us to seek Your wisdom for our lives each day.

If we are to truly understand wisdom, let us experience it in relationships with others, and in our relationship with You. Teach us to weep and to laugh and to love according to divine interpretation.

Whether we attended an Ivy League college or attended the college of life to attain what we know, it is nothing compared to the wisdom the Spirit so generously lavishes upon us when we seek more. Help us to be willing students of Your Spirit today.

In thanks and praise.

Amen.

Our wisdom ought to be nothing else than to embrace with humble teachableness, and at least without finding fault, whatever is taught in Sacred Scripture.

JOHN CALVIN

Such Beautiful Workmanship

*I went down to the potter's house,
and there he was, making something at the
wheel. And the vessel that he made of clay
was marred in the hand of the potter;
so he made it again into another vessel,
as it seemed good to the potter to make.*

JEREMIAH 18:3-4 NKJV

Heavenly Father,
Each day we take for granted the very fact that
we rise from a good night of sleep, stretch out
our arms, rejoice in the aspect of a new day and
listen to the sounds of the morning. We are so
wonderfully made and we enjoy amazing things
that You have given us.

    Help us to recognize that our bodies are
perfectly designed. We have abilities to think and

feel and laugh and cry. We can exercise our judgment and extend our praise. We can do all things because of what You have done.

We thank You, Father, that just as the potter creates worthy vessels, one by one, uniquely and carefully, so You created each of us and saw that we were good. We are incredibly defined and detailed. We are Your workmanship.

Let us take what You have given us and use every breath to Your glory. Let us move with Your Spirit within us to become more of what You would have us be. Mold us, shape us, and renew us according to Your good pleasure, for only You know what perfection we might become.

For every step we take, we thank You.

Amen.

There is about us, if only we have eyes to see, a creation of such spectacular profusion, spendthrift richness, and absurd detail, as to make us catch our breath in astonished wonder.

MICHAEL MAYNE

Welcoming the Warrior Within

*The eyes of the L*ORD *watch over those who do right, and His ears are open to their prayers.*

1 PETER 3:12 NLT

Heavenly Father,

As we strive to become more like You, to offer more of You to those around us, we know that we need to be that much closer to You at all times. We walk around each day wearing the armor of protection and of salvation that You have given us and we proclaim Your name to all who come into our circle of love.

Help us, Lord, to be steadfast warriors. Help us be willing to transform hearts and minds any time we get a chance. Help us to be better servants for the sake of all those who still wait to know more of You. Lord, keep watch over us and fit us for the work that needs to be done. Whether we need to offer a hand or a prayer or a hug, make us willing to do so at any given moment.

We may not always recognize that there's a warrior within us, a fighter ready to take a stand, ready to go into the world and stand firm in our faith for You. Help each of us to win the battles put before us for the good of all of Your children here on earth.

Amen.

God is able to make a way out of no way
and transform dark yesterdays into bright tomorrows.
This is our hope for becoming better people.
This is our mandate for seeking to make a better world.

MARTIN LUTHER KING, JR.

A Woman of Witness

*"If you tell others that you belong to Me,
I will tell My Father in heaven that you
are My followers. But if you reject Me,
I will tell My Father in heaven that
you don't belong to Me."*

MATTHEW 10:32-33 CEV

Heavenly Father,
It is such an honor to be able to shine for You.
We are tiny beams of light casting our rays over a
dark planet that has no light of its own. We are the
moonbeams and You are the Sun.

As opportunities come our way to share the joy,
the hope and the peace that we have found in You,
help us not to worry so much about saying just the
right thing, but help us to be in the moment. Help
us to be a light for You. Help us to be Your arms and
Your eyes and Your hands any time we are called to
do so.

Our sisters before us have helped light the way. Let us follow in the path they have shared and rejoice in the gift You have given us. When we get nervous about how much to say, or how much to pray, or how much to try, then guide our thoughts and our actions for Your good and the good of any who seek You.

Amen.

God has called us to shine. Let no one say that he cannot shine because he has not as much influence as some others may have. What God wants you to do is to use the influence you have.

DWIGHT L. MOODY

Willing to Serve

As for me and my house,
we will serve the LORD.

JOSHUA 24:15 NKJV

Heavenly Father,
It is with humble hearts that we contemplate the idea of serving You. It is awesome to think that there is something we can do to further Your work in the world or give glory to Your name. It is awesome to consider and yet we know that You honor our efforts. You put the "awe" in the things we do so that we even feel good about the "doing".

Lord, help us to serve You better. Help us to serve You with our whole hearts, and our whole bodies, and our whole minds. Help us understand that each thing we do to brighten the spirit of another, lighten the load of someone near or point the way, serves You. Help us crave serving You the same way we crave success and achievement and poetry and sunshine. Let us give the world ease and rescue it in some small way from disease.

Lord, let us come before You in total surrender, ready to respond to whatever need is out there for us to do. Let us shine a light for lost souls and give bread to hungry hearts. Let us serve You in all joy and with great thanksgiving for all You have done for us.

We praise You, dear Lord, and bless Your name.

Amen.

Say well is good, but do well is better;
Do well seems the spirit, say well the letter;
Say well is godly and helps to please,
But do well is godly and gives the world ease.

JOHN OF THE CROSS

Prayerful Worship

"God is Spirit, and those who worship
Him must worship in spirit and truth."

JOHN 4:24 NKJV

Heavenly Father,
We come before You, ready to surrender the weight
of the day, ready to cast off the measure of doubt
that echoes so haphazardly in the spirit, and ready
to renew our hearts and minds in You. We know
that we have not yet worshiped You this day.

Let us come to You for the spiritual food that we
cannot get anywhere else. Let us humbly sit at Your
table and receive from Your bounty, connecting to
Your very Spirit to strengthen and renew our souls.
Lord, feed us the truth so that we may live in the
joy of knowing Your love for us.

Let us step aside as humble beings and rejoice
in the holiness of our Creator. Let us be one with

You and with Jesus Christ. Open our hearts and minds in genuine and conscious worship.

We devote ourselves to Your will. In Jesus' name, we pray.

Amen.

To worship is to quicken the conscience
by the holiness of God, to feed the mind with the
truth of God, to purge the imagination by the
beauty of God, to open the heart to the love of God,
to devote the will to the purpose of God.

WILLIAM TEMPLE

Welcoming Words

*Let the words of Christ live in your hearts and
make you wise. Use His words to teach and
counsel each other. Sing psalms and hymns
and spiritual songs to God with thankful
hearts. And whatever you do or say, let it
be as a representative of the Lord Jesus.*

COLOSSIANS 3:16-17 NLT

Heavenly Father,
We know beyond any doubt what a difference
it makes to us when someone offers kindness
over criticism. We know that keeping Your
words close to our hearts helps us to be kinder
to others and reminds us that each person we
encounter is doing everything possible to
make life work out in a good way.

We come to You today in gratitude for all that You have done to protect and guide and nurture the things we do. We come to You knowing that each time we do, You welcome us back with love and grace and mercy. Help us, Father, to extend that same grace and love to those around us. Help us to be the first with a smile, a kind word or a helping hand.

Our words may fall short of eloquence, but they need never fall short of kindness. Help us to honor Your Spirit in each person who walks the way with us.

Amen.

Kind words can be short and easy to speak,
but their echoes are truly endless.

MOTHER TERESA

The Gift of a Woman's Work

Do your work willingly, as though you were serving the Lord Himself, and not just your earthly master. In fact, the Lord Christ is the one you are really serving, and you know that He will reward you.

COLOSSIANS 3:23-24 CEV

Heavenly Father,
Sometimes we don't have the right perspective about work. We often grumble about the jobs we have and the people we work with and the things that overload us, and totally miss the gifts that You have given us in planting us right smack in the middle of it all. Sometimes we forget that we are there for a purpose and only part of it has anything at all to do with making money or earning a living.

Help us today to see Your hand in our work. Help us to see what You have in mind each time we jump into a new day and take on the tasks at hand. Remind us that You always have work for us to do and that we never have any cause at all to be idle.

As we work with You today, Lord, help us open our eyes to see the treasures You have put in our midst. Help us to see the many ways that our work can further Your work with those around us. Give us the talent and the desire to do our work with the joy of serving You.

Amen.

Thank God every morning when you get up that you have something to do which must be done, whether you like it or not. Being forced to work, and forced to do your best, will breed in you a hundred virtues which the idle never know.

CHARLES KINGSLEY

Without Worry

Jesus said to His disciples,
"Don't be worried! Have faith in God
and have faith in Me."

JOHN 14:1 CEV

Heavenly Father,

Each morning we awaken with full agendas and full helpings of worry before we've even had our first cup of coffee. We often anticipate the day with foreboding, knowing that we can't control the outcomes of all the things we face.

Help us to simply let go. Grant that as we hear the birds sing or the breeze freely winds its way, that we too would trust that wherever we go, You're there and ready to share in all we do.

Help us lay our burdens at Your feet and to go on our way singing Your praises, fully assured that we never walk alone even for an instant.

Thank You, Lord, for watching over our hearts and minds today.

Amen.

"Good morning, theologians!
You wake and sing.
But I, old fool, know less than you
and worry over everything, instead of simply
trusting in the heavenly Father's care."
(Martin Luther, talking to the birds in the woods)
(And the birds sang to Martin Luther …)
"Mortal, cease from toil and sorrow;
God provideth for the morrow."

CHARLES H. SPURGEON

You're an Original!

O LORD, You have searched me and known me.
You know my sitting down and my rising up;
You understand my thought afar off.
You comprehend my path and my lying down,
and are acquainted with all my ways.

PSALM 139:1-3 NKJV

Heavenly Father,

You have created each of us as unique beings. We are known by You in every way and You understand us more than we can actually understand ourselves.

As we imagine what it is that we need to accomplish, and as we try to establish our footing and our direction in the world, we ask that You would guide us. You who know our rising up and our sitting down are the only one qualified to give us advice.

In each of us, You have also planted a thousand outcomes of what we might become. Each of those outcomes is blessed and positive, and each of those outcomes is important. Each step we take, each day we live, brings us closer to all that You intended for us from the very beginning. For only You are acquainted with all our ways.

Help us, Lord, to walk with You, to plant seeds of hope and joy and comfort for those around us, so that we can help to make this earth a joyful garden.

Amen.

The fountain of beauty is the heart,
and every generous thought illustrates
the walls of your chamber.

FRANCIS QUARLES

The Lord's Work

So, my dear sisters,
be strong and steady, always
enthusiastic about the Lord's work,
for you know that nothing you do
for the Lord is ever useless.

1 CORINTHIANS 15:58 NLT

Heavenly Father,
You have graciously surrounded us with remarkable things. We have an abundance of gifts that both serve and distract us. We move beyond them in order to get the work done that You have ordained for us.

Help us to desire the blessing of orderliness. Help us to strive to do all things in a right and decent order so that more people will clearly see our light shine and want that light for themselves.

Help us, Lord, to be strong and steady, step by step, moving along the path of righteousness to claim our inheritance in You and to offer that same inheritance to our sisters everywhere. Help us to bring peace out of the chaos so many face today.

Lord, help us to pay attention to Your people, offering them the steady hand and heart of joy we know through Your Spirit. We ask for this wisdom in Jesus' name.

Amen.

It is our best work that God wants,
not the dregs of our exhaustion.
I think He must prefer quality to quantity.

GEORGE MACDONALD

Being Obedient

"Now if you will obey Me and keep My covenant, you will be My own special treasure from among all the nations of the earth; for all the earth belongs to Me. And you will be to Me a kingdom of priests, My holy nation."

EXODUS 19:5-6 NLT

Heavenly Father,

We know that we fall far short of the mark of true obedience. We know that we walk too often in the ways of the world and sacrifice the things of the spirit. We know we do this because we are often humbled by the very deeds we do and those we know we omitted with weak excuses.

As we learn to trust more, help us to obey more. Help us to set a goal in our own hearts and minds that we will become more mindful of Your will for our lives and that we will joyfully and continually obey.

We long for Your truth, Father, and we know that we are not ready to receive it when we are not poised to obey You even in the small things You have already asked of us. We allow life to cloud our reason and crowd our agendas and we come back to You in weary prayer to confess that we have once more fallen into temptation.

Forgive us for the things that keep us from truly listening, truly giving our hearts to You and truly obeying Your commands. We ask for Your help in becoming more of the treasure You meant for us to be, in Jesus' name.

Amen.

The tiniest fragment of obedience,
and heaven opens up and the profoundest
truths of God are yours straight away. God will
never reveal more truth about Himself till you
obey what you know already.

OSWALD CHAMBERS

Wonderful Opportunities

"So I tell you, keep on asking, and you will be given what you ask for. Keep on looking, and you will find. Keep on knocking, and the door will be opened. For everyone who asks, receives. Everyone who seeks, finds. And the door is opened to everyone who knocks."

LUKE 11:9-10 NLT

Heavenly Father,
We are constantly looking for opportunities to make life better, whether that means making more money, finding more friends, moving to a new place, or some other way.

We know that it is important to seek opportunities to grow and become more of what You would have us be. Help us now as we look for wonderful opportunities to serve You. Grant that we might ask how and when and where we might offer Your grace and Your love to someone else. As often as we ask, bless us with the opportunity.

Lord, help us too to close the doors of regret behind us, knowing that You have already gone on ahead, preparing even greater opportunities for us. Let us not spend so much time looking back that we cannot see the new doors already waiting for us to come up and knock again.

We thank You for the chances that You give us over and over again to ask and receive from Your hand of love and mercy.

Amen.

When one door closes another door opens;
but we often look so long and so regretfully
upon the closed door that we do not see
the one which has opened for us.

ALEXANDER GRAHAM BELL

A Positive Outlook

*Those who are dominated by the sinful
nature think about sinful things, but those
who are controlled by the Holy Spirit
think about things that please the Spirit.*

ROMANS 8:5 NLT

Heavenly Father,
We know what a difference it makes each day
to perceive with a positive spirit and a cheerful
attitude. We know that unexpected blessings
come our way and little miracles seem to happen
without effort. We know, because You have given
each of us a taste of what it's like to see the world
through rose-colored glasses.

By contrast, when we're not willing or able to
see Your gifts that You gently prepared for us,
then we often find ourselves blindsided by events
and storms that we aren't prepared for. We wonder

where You are and why You left us alone and desolate. Yet often, Lord, we know that all that truly happened is that we left You in the dark. We perceived the day with an attitude of foreboding and uncertainty and we got just what we imagined we would.

Help us to look at each day with Your eyes. Help us to hold our thoughts close to Your Holy Spirit so that our attitudes may be transformed into the lightness of being who You intended us to be. We ask this, Lord, in Jesus' name. *Amen.*

The inner attitude of the heart
is far more crucial than the mechanics
for coming into the reality of the spiritual life.

RICHARD FOSTER

An Open
Hand and Heart

He who sows sparingly will also reap sparingly, and he who sows bountifully will also reap bountifully. So let each one give as he purposes in his heart, not grudgingly or of necessity; for God loves a cheerful giver.

2 CORINTHIANS 9:6-7 NKJV

Heavenly Father,
We offer You our hands and our hearts because we understand that all we have comes from You. We look at our friends and neighbors and make an effort to honor them with heartfelt gifts of kindness and answered needs. We thank You for the opportunity You give us to share all that we have with others.

But, Lord, sometimes we forget how much we have and what abundance surrounds us. We don't truly remember that we are constantly in service to each other and we ask You to help us become more generous and gracious givers.

Let us be wise in managing our things and our time, and diligent in opening our hearts and hands to those in need. We have set our hearts on pleasing You. Help us, Lord, to develop an attitude of praise and thanksgiving in the area of sharing our gifts.

Amen.

A cheerful giver does not count the cost of what he gives. His heart is set on pleasing and cheering him to whom the gift is given.

JULIAN OF NORWICH

The Gentle Overseer

*God has given gifts to each of you
from His great variety of spiritual gifts.
Manage them well so that God's
generosity can flow through you.*

1 PETER 4:10 NLT

Heavenly Father,

You have given each of the gifts we need to oversee the welfare of others. We are equipped with Your great mercy on behalf of all who might come into our sphere of influence and need our care.

Help us to use these gifts willingly and lovingly for the good You intended. We know that the things that feel the best to us are often the things that cause us to generously put the needs of others ahead of our own.

As we walk through this week, show us the needs of those around us and grant that we might reach out to them in every possible way. Help us not to withhold our time or our resources. Help us to gently oversee those whose lives we touch in any way.

Bless us with wisdom and with attitudes of great joy in serving others. Help us to truly be the people You know us to be, for the greater good of Your family here on earth. We ask Your help and for a generous infilling of Your Spirit as we go about our daily tasks.

Amen.

Our true worth does not
consist in what human beings think of us.
What we really are is what God knows us to be.

JOHN BERCHMANS

Bless the Little Children

Children are a gift from the Lord;
they are a reward from Him.

PSALM 127:3 NLT

Heavenly Father,
Please bless the children in our homes and those around the world. Grant them good families to be nurtured in and loving communities to grow up in. Give them enough to eat and positive attitudes toward life and learning. Help our children to grow strong and confident and trusting.

Help them to desire more of Your presence in their lives and help us to be good examples of all You have taught us and all that You mean to us.

We are Your children, Lord, and we all need You. Give us wisdom and strength to be the guardians and the guides of our children. If we don't have children of our own, then remind us always to watch over and guard the hearts and minds of children in our families, our churches and our communities, for they are all placed in our care.

Help us to do what we can for children in other countries and other cities, for we know that each child was born with a purpose You meant to have fulfilled. We ask Your help in caring for all of Your children each day.

Amen.

While bringing up your children,
you are to remember that your children
are not your possessions but instead
are the Lord's gift to you.

JOHN C. BROGER

Growing Older

We never give up. Our bodies are gradually dying, but we ourselves are being made stronger each day.

2 CORINTHIANS 4:16 CEV

Heavenly Father,

We have some pretty mixed feelings about getting older. Some part of us regrets the loss of more youthful days, but another part of us enjoys the peace that comes with being a little more relaxed about life. It appears that in Your wisdom, You helped us learn to walk and then run, and then walk again.

Help us to enjoy more fully the days set before us, trusting that You will be with us every step of the way and that You will create more opportunities for many more warm memories.

Remind us of how far we've come, how much we've learned, and how carefully we've grown under Your mercy and care. Let us share our life experiences with those who follow in our footsteps, shining a light to make their way even easier.

Thank You for all that You have taught us and for being with us even unto the end of the age.

Amen.

It would be a good thing if young people
were wise and old people were strong,
but God has arranged things better.

MARTIN LUTHER

Being Reasonable

"Come now, and let us reason together," says the Lord.

ISAIAH 1:18 NKJV

Heavenly Father,

We are constantly learning about what it means to be reasonable people. We want to understand more of life, reason out the things that seem somewhat over the top, and hand our thoughts over to You.

Sometimes, Lord, we spend so much time thinking and looking for reasonable answers that we forget to simply trust that You have all things in Your hand and that we don't really have to bother about all the details. Help us to appreciate the fact that we don't always have to know the "why" of something, even when it doesn't seem reasonable.

Father, our world today often seems scary and

out of control. It feels like we are caught up in national insanity and everything is flip-flopped and overbaked and sour smelling, but we don't know what to do about it. We don't know how to get it back to feeling reasonable again.

We know that You have already gone ahead of us and that You know all the outcomes and will walk with us as we go onward. We believe, Lord, that the most reasonable thing we can do is to follow You. Help us to embrace Your ways and live with a heart of joy. With thanks and praise.

Amen.

We know truth not only by reason
but also by the heart, and it is from this last
that we know first principles.

BLAISE PASCAL

Responsible Women

For it is written: "As I live,
says the Lord, every knee shall bow to Me,
and every tongue shall confess to God."
So then each of us shall give account
of himself to God.

ROMANS 14:11-12 NKJV

Heavenly Father,

We are responsible women, caring about our families and our communities, doing what we can to help those in need and those who suffer unexpected tragedies. We are ever grateful that You are ahead of us, helping to create a new way when a door has closed or directing us on a path that seems hard to find.

We are thankful that the inconsistencies of life can be brought to Your door and that You are already set with a plan to create something new.

As we consider our responsibilities toward our sisters in need and those to whom we owe our devoted attention and care, we ask You to be with us, helping us focus our efforts in caring for those needs that are not just dimly at a distance, but clearly at hand.

Help us to be Your servants wherever we find ourselves, for we know Your children are greatly in need of care. We thank You for all You've provided for us.

Amen.

Our great business in life is not to see what lies dimly at a distance, but to do what lies clearly at hand.

THOMAS CARLYLE

A Woman of Respect

Joshua fell with his face to the ground in reverence. "I am at Your command," Joshua said. "What do You want Your servant to do?" The commander of the LORD's army replied, "Take off your sandals, for this is holy ground." And Joshua did as he was told.

JOSHUA 5:14-15 NLT

Heavenly Father,
Help us to learn from Your servant Joshua. Help us to seek You and honor You and to come into Your presence with a true understanding that we are on holy ground.

Help us to respect the relationship we share with You so much that we would always do "what we are told," even when it sounds like a strange request. Help us to desire to walk in Your ways and

to incline our hearts to see You in all that we
do. As we learn more fully to respect our holy
relationship with You, help us to apply that
respect to each person we meet in Jesus' name.

Amen.

Open my eyes that I may see,
incline my heart that I may desire, order my steps
that I may follow the way of Your commandments.

LANCELOT ANDREWES

Food for the Soul

The heavens declare the glory of God;
the skies proclaim the work of His hands.

PSALM 19:1 NIV

Heavenly Father,
It is with great humility that we observe the
ingenuity and extravagance of Your creation.
The creativity and beauty we see in nature
is astounding: regal mountains, majestic
waterfalls, flower-filled meadows, creatures
and plants of every color, shape and size. The
greatest man-made masterpiece pales into
insignificance when compared with what You
have created.

It is remarkable when we consider how many
types and forms of plants and animals we have
on earth and even more so when we realize that
many of them have not yet even been identified

and named. Every year scientists discover new and previously unknown species.

Every creature, every flower, every mountain stream declares Your glory and sings Your praise. We praise You for providing so many things for our enjoyment. May we truly appreciate Your creativity in every part of creation, whether it be an insect, a spider, a fish, a bird or a flower. Remind us to respect life in all its forms.

Please prompt us to make an effort to spend more time in nature, refreshing our souls and reveling in the beauty You designed and formed.

In Jesus' name, we pray.

Amen.

I love to think of nature as an unlimited broadcasting station, through which God speaks to us every hour, if we will only tune in.

GEORGE WASHINGTON CARVER

A Righteous Woman

He who follows righteousness and mercy finds life, righteousness and honor.

PROVERBS 21:21 NKJV

Heavenly Father,

We don't really understand a word like "righteousness" in the world in which we live. We look at some that we might call "self-righteous" and we know that is not the direction You would have us go.

If we look at righteousness as "right living," then we have a better sense of the word. Help us, then, to live in a way that You would call "right." Help us to get it right more often than we do, so that we can find life and grow in wisdom to honor You more fully.

Help us to understand that our faith in You is the only thing that even gives us a chance to be "right" and so let us be righteous women who are directed, motivated, and firm in our faith toward You in all that we do. We put our hopes for righteousness into Your hands.

Amen.

The righteousness of God is not acquired by acts frequently repeated, as Aristotle taught, but is imparted by faith.

MARTIN LUTHER

Refreshed and Renewed

*Then Jesus said, "Come to Me,
all of you who are weary and carry heavy
burdens, and I will give you rest.
Take My yoke upon you. Let Me teach you,
because I am humble and gentle,
and you will find rest for your souls."*

MATTHEW 11:28-29 NLT

Heavenly Father,
Help us understand that when we give gently and lovingly to others, we are refreshed and renewed in You. Grant that we might give with hearts that are so full of You that we can't help but spill out Your light and mercy and shed Your joy.

Lord, much of the time we go from task to task and feel weary in the running and doing and creating and yet we come away dissatisfied. Remind us that when we are doing Your work and generously giving to others that You have directed us to, that we may indeed feel weary at the end of the day, but we will also feel the fullness of Your Spirit as it washes over us and renews us.

As we learn to shine Your light, bathe us in Your living water, that we might always be ready to give away what we can to uplift those around us. Help us to breathe in Your love and breathe out Your joy. Help us to take Your yoke upon us according to Your desires for us.

Amen.

The purpose of human life is to sense, and to show compassion and the will to help others.

ALBERT SCHWEITZER

Willing to Take a Risk

"Look, I am sending you out as sheep among wolves. Be as wary as snakes and harmless as doves."

MATTHEW 10:16 NLT

Heavenly Father,

We're never certain about when might be the right time to take a risk. We try to weigh all the odds, look at all the parameters of something and then step out when everything looks reasonably secure. We like to walk in a safe zone.

The problem is that much of the time we don't really have that many clues. Sometimes we're forced to risk more than we feel comfortable about. Sometimes we have to garner more faith than we knew we had to make things happen.

We ask, Lord, that You would help us as we step out and risk our hearts, minds and reputations. Please guard and protect our way. Subdue the wolves that would prowl around to take advantage of us and the snakes that attempt to deceive us. Give us Your Spirit of truth and love so that whatever we attempt for You will be accomplished.

Help us not to be content to simply wait and see what will happen when we feel You urging us on to make the right things happen. We ask for Your protection in all that we do.

Amen.

Let us not be content to wait and see
what will happen, but give us the determination
to make the right things happen.

PETER MARSHALL

Sharing Is Caring

"I was hungry, and you fed Me. I was thirsty, and you gave Me a drink. I was a stranger, and you invited Me into your home. I was naked, and you gave Me clothing.
I was sick, and you cared for Me.
I was in prison, and you visited Me."

MATTHEW 25:35-36 NLT

Heavenly Father,
Teach us to share. Show us the ways we can be of service to those in our homes, our communities and our churches. Show us the needs of the broken-hearted, the faint-hearted and the hard-hearted and let us volunteer some food, a glass of water and Your comfort.

   We are Your hands and Your feet on this earth, Lord, and we are blessed to do Your work. Help us to apply ourselves lovingly and joyfully to those around us in whatever way we are called to their side. Let us shine Your light into their veil of darkness and refresh their spirits.

In all that we do this week, Father, open our eyes to every need and let us reach out in Your love. We ask this in Your mercy.

Amen.

Here is the truly Christian life, here is
faith really working by love: When a woman
applies herself with joy and love to the works
of that freest servitude, in which she serves
others voluntarily and for naught;
herself abundantly satisfied in the fullness
and richness of her own faith.

ADAPTED FROM MARTIN LUTHER

Harmony

*Nothing exists that He didn't make.
Life itself was in Him, and this life
gives light to everyone. The light
shines through the darkness, and the
darkness can never extinguish it.*

JOHN 1:3-5 NLT

Heavenly Father,

Thank You for giving us Your Divine Light.
Thank You for helping us to see our way
through the darkness. Grant that we might
serve each other in kindness, radiating Your
Spirit to those who come into our presence.

Lord, lead us to the places where Your light
is needed. Give us courage to shine even when
it is not easy to do so.

Bring harmony into our homes and into

our hearts so that we might become part of the solution for harmony in our nation. Our country and our world are in deep need of Your magnificent light. Help us this week to shine for You in everything we do.

Amen.

If there is light in the soul,
there will be beauty in the person.
If there is beauty in the person,
there will be harmony in the house.
If there is harmony in the house,
there will be order in the nation.
If there is order in the nation,
there will be peace in the world.

PROVERB

Sing and Shout

I celebrate and shout because of My Lord God. His saving power and justice are the very clothes I wear. They are more beautiful than the jewelry worn by a bride or a groom. The Lord will bring about justice and praise in every nation on earth, like flowers blooming in a garden.

ISAIAH 61:10-11 CEV

Heavenly Father,

We sing and shout to You for dressing us in cloaks of saving power and justice. We know that You are in control and that You reign in all the universe.

Even when the world despairs of evildoers and cataclysmic forces of nature that destroy the homes and the lives of some of Your children, we know that You are the victor.

We know that You will work miracles in as many lives each day as You possibly can so that great works can be accomplished and we thank You for that. We ask that You would grant us the blessing of Your protection, and Your saving power and mercy in every step we take this week. We ask that You would bring healing to our dark planet and turn our deeds to light and growth and joy. We thank You and praise You with every aspect of our being, in the name of Jesus.

Amen.

If anyone would tell you the shortest, surest way to all happiness and all perfection, he must tell you to make a rule to yourself to thank and praise God in everything that happens to you. For it is certain that whatever seeming calamity happens to you, if you thank and praise God for it, you turn it into a blessing. If you could work miracles, therefore, you could not do more for yourself than by this thankful spirit. It heals with a word, and turns all that it touches into happiness.

WILLIAM LAW

You Are Remarkable!

The wisdom that comes from above
leads us to be pure, friendly, gentle, sensible,
kind, helpful, genuine, and sincere.

JAMES 3:17 CEV

Heavenly Father,
We are often fooled into thinking that being "remarkable" has something to do with recognition for a talent or a skill. We think that it might be attached to those who we see on the big screen or those who enter into politics. Help us to see that we are defined by the remarkable things we do for You.

We are Your children and we are remarkable each time we lift up someone in need who walks beside us. We are remarkable each time we share Your love with someone who was just waiting for us to open that door.

Remind us, Lord, as we work through our endless chores this week that the duties that occupy our time at home or at work or anywhere else can become heavenly ones if we do them for You. We might just discover that what we have done is simply remarkable because it is stamped with Your love and approval.

Bless each of us as we step out in the wisdom of love and genuine kindness to create a brighter day for someone else. Help us live for You today.

Amen.

One thing, and only one, in this world has eternity stamped upon it. Feelings pass; resolves and thoughts pass; opinions change. What you have done lasts – lasts in you. Through ages, through eternity, what you have done for Christ, that, and only that, you are.

F. W. ROBERTSON

Becoming True-Hearted

"The Spirit shows what is true and will come and guide you into the full truth."

JOHN 16:13 CEV

Heavenly Father,
Help us become true-hearted women. Help us to desire to live Your truth in front of others in the world and to share Your truth as we understand it. Grant us Your Spirit of Truth to guide all that we do and to enlighten us according to the steps You would have us take.

As we seek greater understanding, Father, help us to shed the cloaks of fear and uncertainty that sometimes prevent us from seeing what is really true for us. Clothe us, instead, with Your love and kindness and patience so that we can meet the needs of those around us and offer them loving and willing hearts of joy.

We come before You knowing that there is much to learn as we attempt to become more fully aware of Your truths even within ourselves. We ask that You would purge us of ideas that hide in our minds and hearts that are not of You.

Release Your Holy Spirit within us to cleanse and renew us into all truth, that we might serve You better. Grace us with Your favor, Lord, according to Your divine intention for all that we do.

Amen.

If you don't learn and know your truths,
you cannot speak them. If you don't speak them,
you will know a prison within.
Tell your truths to yourself, and then to others.
The truth really will set you free!

ANONYMOUS

Devoted Hearts

Be earnest and disciplined in your prayers. Most important of all, continue to show deep love for each other, for love covers a multitude of sins. Cheerfully share your home with those who need a meal or a place to stay.

1 PETER 4:7-9 NLT

Heavenly Father,

As we aspire to understand more of Your truth, let our actions fully reflect what we have because of You. We don't know how long it will be before You come again and the world as we know it is forever changed.

We know, therefore, that the work must continue and that our hearts must be right before You to get it accomplished. We offer our love and our service.

We offer that our devoted hearts and minds to take the action of encouraging those around us and furthering Your kingdom.

Lord, we ask too that You help us to more fully dedicate ourselves to prayer so that we might learn to trust and obey You in all things, regardless of what is changing in our lives or happening in the world around us.

We ask that You would increase the size of our hearts so that we are more loving and more generous than we have ever been. Let us not even recognize ourselves as we normally are, but become truly devoted to Your Spirit and the work to be done. For each deed we undertake for the good of others, we ask Your blessing. In the name of Your Son, we pray.

Amen.

A thousand words will not leave so
deep an impression as one deed.

HENRIK IBSEN

As a Woman Thinks

*Therefore if there is any consolation
in Christ, fulfill my joy by being like-minded,
having the same love, being of one accord,
of one mind. Let nothing be done through
selfish ambition or conceit. Let each of you
look out not only for his own interests,
but also for the interests of others.*

PHILIPPIANS 2:1-4 NKJV

Heavenly Father,

We know that our thoughts are not aligned with Your thoughts. We know that we are in continual need of guidance, especially so when it comes to the things that we think about.

Lord, so often ideas and images show up on the blackboards of our minds without us even knowing how they got there. Help us to examine those things that confuse and discourage us and erase the ones that are not of You.

Rewrite Your truth in ways that will keep us strong and faithful.

Grant that we might be of one mind concerning the needs of those around us. Help us esteem others and value them with an understanding heart and an open mind. Help us to respect those who think or act differently than we do.

Help us to be willing to serve everyone who walks into our sphere of influence. Let our most generous thoughts be for the highest good of each person we meet. Help us, Lord, to think thoughts of love everywhere we go.

Amen.

Watch your thoughts; they become words.
Watch your words; they become actions.
Watch your actions; they become habits.
Watch your habits; they become character.
Watch your character; for it becomes your destiny.

ANONYMOUS

Students and Teachers

*"Whom will he teach knowledge?
And whom will he make to understand the
message? Those just weaned from
milk? Those just drawn from the breasts? For
precept must be upon precept, precept upon
precept, line upon line, line upon
line, here a little, there a little."*

ISAIAH 28:9-10 NKJV

Heavenly Father,
We come to You as both students and teachers.
We desire to learn all that we can at Your feet
so that we may have greater understanding
and wisdom to share with others. We welcome
Your instruction and Your demonstrations of
kindness and creativity in our lives.

We recognize that we do not always get each lesson right when we're at Your feet and that often You must show us more than once what You would have us know.

Remind us as we share Your Word with others that we need to give them the same grace that You so continually give us. Help us to be teachers who not only tell and explain, but demonstrate the truth You have given us in our lives every day.

Help us to be witnesses to Your light in the world and grant that we might inspire the desire in others to come to know more of You.

We ask You these things, Lord, according to Your mercy and grace.

Amen.

The mediocre teacher tells.
The good teacher explains.
The superior teacher demonstrates.
The great teacher inspires.

WILLIAM A. WARD

Days of Temptation

*God blesses the people who patiently
endure testing. Afterward they will receive
the crown of life that God has promised to
those who love Him. No one who wants to do
wrong should ever say, "God is tempting me."
God is never tempted to do wrong, and He
never tempts anyone else either. Temptation
comes from the lure of our own evil desires.*

JAMES 1:12-14 NLT

Heavenly Father,
We confess that we are often drawn into
temptation. Sometimes these temptations
seem innocent enough, one more piece
of chocolate or one tiny white lie to save
someone's feelings.

Sometimes we're so sure that we can't be
tempted by the really big sins that we find
ourselves falling into those traps without
realizing what we've done. Sometimes, Lord,

we even succumb to those temptations and our hearts break with the sorrow of knowing we have let You down.

Help us to meditate more carefully on Your Word and to strive to keep those words ever present in our hearts. Grant that we might resist on the days of temptation and win the battle, no matter how insignificant it may seem. You know us, Father, and You know what trips us up.

Help us to be willing to truthfully face the things that tempt us so that we can arm ourselves against another failure should that very temptation come our way once more. Help us always to draw closer to You, that we may overcome the desires for things that take us from the path of salvation.

Amen.

The voice of Christ: Write My words in your heart and meditate on them earnestly, for in time of temptation they will be very necessary.

THOMAS À KEMPIS

Count Your Blessings

*It is good to give thanks to the Lord,
to sing praises to the Most High.
It is good to proclaim Your unfailing
love in the morning, Your faithfulness
in the evening. You thrill me, Lord,
with all You have done for me! I sing
for joy because of what You have done.*

PSALM 92:1-2, 4 NLT

Heavenly Father,
What a joy it is to come before You with a heart
of grateful praise! So many times we seek You
because life has assailed us with heartache
or worry and we need Your comfort and Your
guidance. We need to know that You are ever in
control and that all things regarding our well-
being are in Your hand.

Knowing You are there for us is one of the reasons we shout for joy. It is one of the reasons we awaken to each new day with glad hearts and willing minds. You give us unending gifts and all we have to do is to look for them.

Help us this week to discover Your mercies hidden in the kindness of another person's encouragement, echoed in the sound of a melodious bird, or revealed in a breathtaking sunrise. Help us to count our many blessings every morning and every evening and sing for joy!

Amen.

The more we look for them, the more of them we will see. Better to lose count while naming your blessings than to lose your blessings to counting your troubles.

MALTBIE D. BABCOCK

Spiritual Gifts

A spiritual gift is given to each of
us so we can help each other.

1 CORINTHIANS 12:7 NLT

Heavenly Father,
You have blessed us with a variety of talents and
abilities to use in getting work done, in raising
children, in creating our home environments.
You have shown us how to use our gifts and
You have given us instruction to share our best
efforts with those around us.

   Lord, help us to remain talented women.
Help us to have the talent to see when someone
needs a helping hand. Help us develop the
talent to offer a smile or a warm hug at just the
right moment. Give us the wisdom to overcome
the obstacles that keep us from being all that
You have designed us so carefully to be. Remind

us that You are not done in developing talents within us and that there are more gifts to be discovered in each one of us.

Help us not to be afraid to try new things and grow in new ways to serve You. Thank You for making each of us shine in our own unique way and for giving us so many opportunities to be talented and shining stars.

Amen.

The more I see of the real champions and succeeders in this world, the more I become convinced that natural aptitude and talent are not the secrets to their success. Rather it is the ability to overcome obstacles, that makes the difference between success and failure.

ROBERT BACKMAN

Tender Talk

*Timely advice is as lovely as
golden apples in a silver basket.*

PROVERBS 25:11 NLT

Heavenly Father,
Golden apples in a silver basket offer us a beautiful image as we consider the ways that we speak to one another. If we were busy handing out golden apples to each other, we'd no doubt find the world a much more pleasant place to be.

Of course, we know that it's important to not only be pleasant, but when it's necessary, we must be willing to give advice with a loving heart and in a timely manner.

Some of us feel reluctant to give advice and yet any words that are offered in love, kindness and a true spirit of caring must be somewhat like apples of gold.

Help us, Father, to share the kindest words we can to instill faith and confidence and hope in others. Help us to fill their silver baskets with as many golden apples as we can, always picking the most ripe and beautiful words available to us.

Help us to nurture the hearts and minds of all those we meet this week so that they will grow in their desire to know more of You. Let our kind words produce good fruit.

Amen.

Kindness is the language which the deaf can hear and the blind can see.

MARK TWAIN

One Tough Woman

He will keep you strong to the end,
so that you will be free from all blame on
the day when our Lord Jesus Christ returns.

1 CORINTHIANS 1:8 NLT

Heavenly Father,

You are our strength. It is You who gives us the stamina to try again when we think we have tried every possible door. It is You who reminds us that we're not alone when we feel that we're carrying the burdens of the world. You lift us up again and strengthen our resolve to take another look, try another path, meet another challenge.

If any would call us strong, then we are grateful. We know that sometimes we look much stronger than we feel and that we try to act stronger than our belief in what is happening around us. Though our belief in certain ideas or situations may falter, our faith does not.

We are steadfast in You and we hang on to Your promises and Your goodness and Your plans for our lives. We rest in You, Lord, remembering that in Your time, You will raise us up past any obstacle we face. We pray with hearts of thanksgiving.

Amen.

Be of good cheer.
Do not think of today's failures,
but of the success that may come tomorrow.
You have set yourselves a difficult task,
but you will succeed if you persevere;
and you will find joy in overcoming obstacles.
Remember, no effort that we make
to attain something beautiful is ever lost.

HELEN KELLER

Being Trustworthy

*I will say of the Lord, "He is my refuge
and my fortress, my God, in whom I trust."*

PSALM 91:2 NIV

Heavenly Father,
It is no easy task for us to learn to trust. We have
trusted in our youth, only to have that trust
destroyed by deceit or foolishness. We have
trusted those we thought would always stand
beside us, only to discover that they would
indeed let us down in the right circumstances.
Yet we know that You are the example of real
trust and we strive to emulate You in the way
that others can learn to trust us.

Help us to become worthy women of trust
who consider it a great failing to ever break
a respected agreement with someone else.

Help us to grow in Your Spirit so that we can be strengthened and renewed in that process of becoming more trustworthy.

As we face the future, Father, help us to trust all things in our lives to You, our Divine Keeper and Protector.

Amen.

Do not look forward to the changes and the chances of this life in fear; rather look to them with full hope that, as they arise, God, whose you are, will deliver you out of them. He is your Keeper. He has kept you hitherto. Do you but hold fast to His dear hand, and He will lead you safely through all things; and, when you cannot stand, He will bear you in His arms.

FRANCIS DE SALES

Spiritually and Gracefully Helpful

I will lift up my eyes to the hills –
from whence comes my help? My help
comes from the Lord, who made heaven
and earth. He will not allow your foot
to be moved; He who keeps you will not
slumber. Behold, He who keeps Israel
shall neither slumber nor sleep.

PSALM 121:1-4 NKJV

Heavenly Father,

Sometimes we don't really know what it means to be helpful. We dash into doing things that we assume will be right, only to discover that we totally missed what was needed, what was truly helpful.

Direct our thoughts and actions to the real needs of those around us, so that our helpfulness can be genuinely useful and reflective of Your love and grace. When we are uncertain of the steps to take, remind us to look to You, as the psalmist said so long ago. Where else can any of us get help except from You?

Be with us now, Lord, as we go through the week and grant us wisdom in the little things. Show us the simple ways where we can lend a hand, offer a kindness or encouragement, or stick our necks out in the ways that are truly beneficial to others.

We know that on any given day, we too may need those things right back. Let us be women who are spiritually and graciously helpful.

Amen.

Giving is the secret of a healthy life.
Not necessarily money, but whatever a person has
of encouragement and sympathy and understanding.

JOHN D. ROCKEFELLER, JR.

A Humble Heart

Humble yourselves under the mighty power of God, and in His good time He will honor you. Give all your worries and cares to God, for He cares about what happens to you.

1 PETER 5:6-7 NLT

Heavenly Father,

We recognize that humility is not always our strongest suit. We know how easily we place ourselves in a position of authority, forgetting for the moment that no matter what we know or what we have, that You have been the Giver and the Gift.

Sometimes we make assumptions about others, judging circumstances or situations without the benefit of truth or knowledge of the real story. We cast our judgments without true humility and we ask Your forgiveness for that.

Lord, as we approach this week, remind us that when we humble ourselves before You, we widen the opportunity for You to do good in our lives and in the lives of others. We offer ourselves to do Your work, honoring You in all that we do and sharing the gifts divinely created in each of us.

In praise and blessing, we thank You.

Amen.

"The humble soul knows that all
that she is and every gift she has is from Me,
not from herself, and to Me she attributes all."

CATHERINE OF SIENA

(HEARING GOD SPEAK IN A VISION)

The Gift of Laughter

If you are cheerful, you feel good;
if you are sad, you hurt all over.

PROVERBS 17:22 CEV

Heavenly Father,
Remind us of how important it is to always have a sense of humor. Sometimes we get so caught up in the issues of life that we make everything seem serious and forget to laugh.

Help us to renew and refresh ourselves with little mirth breaks to ease the tensions and the stress, feeding our weary spirits during the day. Strengthen our friendships and special relationships with sustainable smiles and cheerful attitudes.

Lord, as we go through the week ahead, show us the gifts of laughter that help heal difficulties and encourage friendships to grow.

Help us to be more than the helping hands and the serious students of Your Word. Help us to be ambassadors of joy, because we know that we have You to lift our spirits whenever we put our worries at Your feet. Grant us many reasons to smile this week.

Amen.

Humor is the great thing,
the saving thing. The minute it crops up,
all our irritations and resentments slip
away and a sunny spirit takes their place.

MARK TWAIN

Filled with Hope

*My prayer is that light will flood
your hearts and that you will understand
the hope that was given to you when
God chose you. Then you will discover
the glorious blessings that will be yours
together with all of God's people.*

EPHESIANS 1:18 CEV

Heavenly Father,
We are definitely women of hope. We put our
hope in You, our faith in You and our very being
into Your hands. As we walk our various life
paths, we walk them knowing that no matter
what we do for a living, where we are in our
understanding of faith, or how much we have
grown in spirit, we are grounded in the hope
You have given us in Jesus Christ.

We know that nothing else can take that hope from us, for it is Your eternal gift and we are grateful.

Lord, grant that we might keep our hopes high this week and share the light of our hope with those around us. Help us to be the messengers of encouragement in the lives of others every chance we get and to be the light You have created us to be.

We praise You for choosing us to be Your daughters and we ask that You would bless our hopes for those we love in every area of life according to Your will and purpose.

Amen.

Those who keep speaking about the sun while walking under a cloudy sky are messengers of hope, the true saints of our day.

HENRI J. NOUWEN

An Honest Woman

"Now if you walk before Me as your father David walked, in integrity of heart and in uprightness, to do according to all that I have commanded you, and if you keep My statutes and My judgments, then I will establish the throne of your kingdom over Israel forever."

1 KINGS 9:4-5 NKJV

Heavenly Father,

We want to be honest with You and walk with integrity of heart. We want that, but we know that we do not always achieve such honesty. We give ourselves plausible reasons to accept compromise and we do it without even fully understanding why.

Please help us to be upright, considerate and truthful in the things that we do. Help us not to slip into temptation over little things, or let minor offences become too important. Grant that we may be more honest about our willingness to be forgiving. We know, Father, that You care about all we do, and not so much from the view of catching us in sin, but from the view of helping us see the truth.

As we grow in Your love and guidance, may we walk before You as our ancestor David did, truly owning the things that we do, confessing our sins, and loving You with our whole heart and mind.

Amen.

Our lives improve only when we take chances –
and the first and most difficult risk we
can take is to be honest with ourselves.

WALTER ANDERSON

Shaped by the Heart

*"Your words show what is in your hearts.
Good people bring good things out
of their hearts, but evil people bring
evil things out of their hearts."*

MATTHEW 12:34-35 CEV

Heavenly Father,
We offer You our hearts and ask that You would shape them and mold them and create them to become even more of what You would have us be.

We know that every thought, every gift, every attitude is shaped by the heart. We know that we strive to be good women who offer only good things from the bottom of our hearts. We make every effort to set Your light on a lampstand for everyone to see.

Whatever treasures we have gained by Your grace and goodness, we know that nothing is to be treasured like Your love. Melt our hearts each day so that more of Your love is revealed to the world and more of Your goodness comes from our mouths. Help us to always bring kind words to those around us.

Amen.

You must keep all earthly treasures
out of your heart, and let Christ be your treasure,
and let Him have your heart.

CHARLES H. SPURGEON

A Woman of Humanity

*You are the one who put me together
inside my mother's body, and I praise You
because of the wonderful way You created
me. Everything You do is marvelous!
Of this I have no doubt.*

PSALM 139:13-14 CEV

Heavenly Father,

We cannot step aside from our humanity and
call ourselves followers of Christ. We know that
each time we wipe a tear, feed a hungry child,
comfort the sick and applaud the joyful, we are
showing our humanity.

You created us to first and foremost be
good and kind and loving human beings. You
surrounded us with examples of how You would
have us treat each other and You gave us the
golden rule.

We know that things improve remarkably when we treat others in as thoughtful and as loving a way as we hope to be treated in return.

Though we often feel discouraged at the news and the times in which we live, we recognize that we are part of the solution. When we follow Your will, desire and plan for our lives, we bring forward a spiritual antidote to offset the destruction we hear about each day in the media. Help us to step up and be counted as a change for good.

In the name of Jesus, we pray.

Amen.

In helping others, we help ourselves.

WOODROW KROLL

Be Holy

*But now you must be holy in everything
you do, just as God – who chose you
to be His children – is holy. For He
Himself has said, "You must be holy
because I am holy."*

1 PETER 1:15-16 NLT

Heavenly Father,
We don't really understand holiness. It feels like
something unattainable, something that is so
completely from You that we can't even imagine
how we can come close to it. Yet the truth is
that we can only come close to it because You
opened the door with the birth, life, death and
resurrection of Your Son. He taught us about
holiness and helped us understand that through
Him we too can be holy.

We thank You that as our relationship grows more mature and our faith more yielding, we can begin to see the beauty of striving for holiness. Help us to desire more of You and less of ourselves so that we can shine a holy light on the needs of the world. Help us to point the way to Your Son, Jesus.

As we move through another week, show us the ways in which we can return holy moments to You. With praise and thanksgiving, we call on Your Holy Spirit.

Amen.

Holiness involves friendship with God. There has to be a moment in our relationship with God when He ceases to be just a Sunday acquaintance and becomes a weekday friend.

BASIL HUME

Living in Harmony

We are partners working together for God.

1 CORINTHIANS 3:9 CEV

Heavenly Father,
It's not always easy for us to be at peace with the circumstances and events of our lives. We seek harmony and yet often find ourselves in chaos. We look for the good in others, only to be disappointed in the complex personalities and misunderstandings we have to deal with.

We realize, Lord, that the ego is a strong force in the world that often brings disharmony. Most of us don't even realize how often we battle the ego, our own, or someone else's. Help us to seek understanding. Help us to seek truth and to find ways to sit down and work out our differences.

Nothing is more valuable to us than having

Your peace, Father. In a world that offers us too many choices, too many variables, too many fears, we are even more aware of the precious moments when we can live in Your grace and Your peace.

Grant us wisdom in the ways we deal with others and let us seek harmony and truth above all things. We know that from those things, we serve in love.

Amen.

It is understanding that gives us an ability to have peace. When we understand the other person's viewpoint, and receive understanding of our own, then we can sit down and work out our differences.

HARRY S. TRUMAN (ADAPTED)

Good Habits

"No one knows the day or hour when these things will happen, not even the angels in heaven or the Son Himself. Only the Father knows. And since you don't know when they will happen, stay alert and keep watch."

MARK 13:32-33 NLT

Heavenly Father,
We know we need to pay closer attention to those things that have become habits in our lives. Some of them are simple, like sitting in the same pew every week at church or ordering the same meal every time we go to our favorite restaurant.

Some of them are not so simple, like giving up smoking or forming better eating habits, and yet we are the living products of all our choices. Help us to acquire those habits that are easy to live with, not only for us, but for those who live around us. Help us to become the kind of people that others want to be around because we habitually do good things.

We don't know, Lord, when You will return for us. We only know that we must continue in the habits of prayer, giving, loving and being all that You want us to be, because that is why You created us.

Help us to stay alert to all that we can do to build more beneficial habits in our work for You.

Amen.

Good habits are hard to acquire but easy to live with.
Bad habits are easy to acquire but hard to live with.

ANONYMOUS

Understanding Happiness

A merry heart makes a cheerful countenance.

PROVERBS 15:13 NKJV

Heavenly Father,
We know that emotional happiness is
somewhat fleeting. It comes and goes with
the circumstances of our lives and sometimes
without true recognition on our part.

We know that the gift of happiness has a lot
to do with our perceptions of life that align with
Your purpose for us. When we are working in
alignment with You, we have a sense of well-
being, and peace and happiness results. When
we are at odds with Your purpose, it doesn't
really matter what we do, happiness eludes us.
Help us to seek "holy" happiness. Help us to
desire more of those things that create harmony
and peace and a sense of joy in all that we do.

Lord, we also realize that those who say that people are about as happy as they "think" they are have a valid point.

Create in us a true desire to reflect the happiness we genuinely feel in the warm embrace of our families and friends and those who wish all good things for us. We know we have many good reasons to feel happy and we thank You for every one of them.

Amen.

Many persons have a wrong idea
of what constitutes true happiness.
It is not attained through self-gratification
but through fidelity to a worthy purpose.

HELEN KELLER

A Woman of Hospitality

*Remember this – a farmer who plants
only a few seeds will get a small crop.
But the one who plants generously will get a
generous crop. You must each make up your
own mind as to how much you should give.
For God loves the person who gives cheerfully.
And God will generously provide all you need.*

2 CORINTHIANS 9:6-8 NLT

Heavenly Father,
We know that we must be women who open
our hearts and minds and homes and hands to
those in need around us. We see Your people in
our neighborhoods and across our communities.
We see Your people around the world and we
know they need to be fed and clothed and taken
care of.

Sometimes, we see so many people, Lord, that we feel overwhelmed about how to take care of them all.

Help us remember that even when we can't get involved in every cause and every need, we can get involved in some. We can help one person who needs a listening ear or encouragement. We can help another person by offering a meal or a good winter coat. We can help in any number of ways and we believe that's what You ask of us.

Make us aware of those who need us in some way in our own backyards. Give us willing hearts and hospitable arms of welcome. We only offer to others what You have so graciously already given us. We thank You for Your incredible hospitality.

Amen.

We should give as we would receive, cheerfully, quickly, and without hesitation; for there is no grace in a benefit that sticks to the fingers.

SENECA

A Gift from God

"All your children will be taught by the Lord, and great will be their peace."

ISAIAH 54:13 NIV

Heavenly Father,
We come to You today to thank You for the blessing of children. Though they may drive us wild sometimes, life would be empty without them. Our children make us feel complete: a family.

We pray for Your protection and blessing on our children today. Reassure us that all is well, and that You have Your hand upon them, guiding them and revealing Your truth to them.

Help us never to take our children for granted, and to cherish each and every day with them. Help us to appreciate each one's unique personality and to play our part in growing them into who You intended them to be.

You entrusted these precious souls into our care; please help us to be good examples, good role models for them to follow. Let our lives reflect Your love and help us to be conscious of this. In the hustle and bustle of every day, remind us of the special calling to be mothers and that there is no more important task in the whole world.

In Your precious name.

Amen.

Only God Himself fully appreciates the influence of a Christian mother in the molding of character in her children.

BILLY GRAHAM

A Work in Progress

You are members of God's family. Together, we are His house, built on the foundation of the apostles and the prophets. And the cornerstone is Christ Jesus Himself.

EPHESIANS 2:19-20 NLT

Heavenly Father,

Marriage was Your idea, a partnership You created, knowing how important it is to form a bond and to be part of a family. Today we bring our marriages to You, asking for Your blessing and Your strength to help us see them through. We place our husbands before You and prayerfully request that You would encourage and build them up in all areas of their lives: work, fatherhood, relationship with You, friendships and marriage.

We thank You for bringing us through all the storms and difficult times. We know that we will stand strong if we include You in our marriages, even though it may not be plain sailing. I pray that our friendships with our husbands may not dim in the hum drum of work, housework and kids.

Please help us to always respect and love our husbands, even when we may not feel he deserves it. Likewise, we pray for love, patience and kindness towards us, even when we may be unloving.

We thank You, Lord, for granting these and other blessings.

Amen.

There is no more lovely, friendly or charming relationship, communion or company, than a good marriage.

MARTIN LUTHER

Every Life Is Precious

Ask the animals, and they will teach you,
or the birds in the sky, and they will tell you;
or speak to the earth, and it will teach you,
or let the fish in the sea inform you.
Which of all these does not know
that the hand of the LORD has done this?
In His hand is the life of every creature
and the breath of all mankind.

JOB 12:7-10 NIV

Heavenly Father,

We know that in Your mighty wisdom, You created all the animals on earth: every bird, every reptile, every insect, every fish, every mammal, and every spider. There is so much we can learn from them, about provision, loyalty, respect, purpose, love, freedom and joy. Let us take these lessons to heart as we observe the interactions in the world around us.

Please help us to shed our preconceptions and fears about animals and to treat each one with respect, knowing that it was created by You. Where there is a need for care, love, food or a home, please prompt us to not stand by, but to stand up for Your creatures, who so often have no voice.

May we never negate to care for the environment in all the small ways we can, such as separating waste and recycling, not being wasteful, and being conscious of what purchases we make.

Thank You, Father, for helping us to be more responsible caretakers of Your beautiful world.

Amen.

A man is truly ethical only when he obeys the compulsion to help all life which he is able to assist, and shrinks from injuring anything that lives.

ALBERT SCHWEITZER

The Lord Restores Your Soul

The LORD is my shepherd; I shall not want.
He makes me to lie down in green pastures;
He leads me beside the still waters.
He restores my soul.

PSALM 23:1-3 NKJV

Heavenly Father,

In this busy world, it seems like the days fly by in a whirlwind of work, caring for our families, household responsibilities and other tasks. In this busyness, we know that it is even more important to start the day with You. You give us strength and encouragement for each new day, reminding us of our purpose and of the incredible truth that You are always beside us.

Help us to live each moment conscious of Your presence, knowing that we can talk to You at any time. Please remind us of the importance of having a quiet time with You, when it is just the two of us.

We know that we also need to set aside some "me time", whether it is enjoying a cup of tea in the garden, having a relaxing bubble bath, or going for a walk in the neighborhood. Thank You for refreshing us and for giving us the courage to live fully for You each and every day.

Amen.

As long as I am content to know that He is infinitely greater than I, and that I cannot know Him unless He shows Himself to me, I will have peace, and He will be near me and in me, and I will rest in Him.

THOMAS MERTON

KAREN MOORE

Karen is the author of more than
60 books for both children and adults.
She has a Master's degree in education
and is a teacher, writer and speaker.
Karen is the mother of three grown
children and lives in sunny Florida.